Little Squire

True HORSE Stories

Little Squire

THE JUMPING PONY

BY JUDY ANDREKSON

Illustrations by David Parkins

Tundra Books

Text copyright © 2007 by Judy Andrekson
Illustrations copyright © 2007 by David Parkins

Published in Canada by Tundra Books,
75 Sherbourne Street, Toronto, Ontario M5A 2P9

Published in the United States by Tundra Books of Northern New York,
P.O. Box 1030, Plattsburgh, New York 12901

Library of Congress Control Number: 2006925472

Library and Archives Canada Cataloguing in Publication
Andrekson, Judy
Little Squire : the jumping pony / Judy Andrekson ; illustrated by
David Parkins.

(True horse stories)
ISBN 978-0-88776-770-8

1. Little Squire (Horse)–Juvenile literature. 2. Show jumpers
(Horses)–Biography–Juvenile literature. 3. Connemara
pony–Biography–Juvenile literature. 4. Ponies–United
States–Biography–Juvenile literature. I. Parkins, David
II. Title. III. Series.

SF295.565.L58A54 2007   j798.2'50929   C2006-902062-0

ONTARIO ARTS COUNCIL
CONSEIL DES ARTS DE L'ONTARIO

We acknowledge the financial support of the Government of Canada through the
Book Publishing Industry Development Program (BPIDP) and that of the
Government of Ontario through the Ontario Media Development Corporation's
Ontario Book Initiative. We further acknowledge the support of the Canada
Council for the Arts and the Ontario Arts Council for our publishing program.

This book is printed on acid-free paper that is 100% recycled,
ancient-forest friendly (40% post-consumer recycled).

Printed and bound in Canada

2 3 4 5 6   19 18 17 16

For Laura and Kari, who had to wait so long,
John, who gives so much,
and for my most special girl,
Kate.

Acknowledgments

I would like to express my sincerest gratitude to the many wonderful people who shared their memories with me as I researched this story. Thank you to Dr. Donal Corry, son of Captain Dan Corry, and Mary O'Rourke, daughter of Jim Rice, for sharing your fathers with me. Thanks to Betty Shea, widow of Danny Shea, for your remembrances. Thanks so much to Audrey Colgan and Joanie and Eddie Hogan, daughters and son-in-law of Mickey Walsh, for braving the computer and offering so much. And a very special thanks to Phoebe Walsh-Robertson, youngest daughter of Mickey and Kitty Walsh, for your unending enthusiasm for this project and for continuing to dig deeper. Sharing these memories of your incredible father with you has been incredibly touching and I am so grateful to you for offering this to me.

Contents

I

An Ocean Apart

Mickey Walsh dreamed about going to America. To Irish boys like him, America was known as the Land of Opportunity. People said that the streets were paved with gold, and any boy or man could find work there and become someone special. Nearly every family Mickey knew had someone who had left in recent years and he wanted to go, too.

Mickey thought of all the stories he had heard about America as he cleaned the stalls in his father's stable. He talked endlessly about it with his brothers as they settled

for the night in the room above their parents' pub, The Corner House, awaiting sleep. He listened raptly anytime the pub's visitors brought up the topic. He planned what he would do if he ever got to America, and saved his money for the trip he knew he would one day take.

The Corner House Pub and its stable yard of about twenty stuccoed, stone box stalls was, and is still, located on the crossroads of a small, scenic town called Kildorrey, in the southwest region of Ireland. Kildorrey is in County Cork on the crest of one of the many rolling hills of the area. From the top of the stone steps that led from the boys' room down to the stable yard, a person could see for miles. Each morning, Mickey began his day with a beautiful view of rich green grasslands, gentle hills, and wooded valleys spread before him in the sweet freshness of the moist, mild climate. Below, his father's horses nickered their impatience to be fed and turned out. Mickey felt impatient, too.

Mickey's parents, Thomas and Hannah Walsh, ran the pub and the stable with the help of their nine children – six boys and three girls. Mickey's father was an avid horseman, and his exceptional skills in horse-trading, riding, and horsemanship had been passed on to the Walsh children. Mickey was an eager student and a true lover of horses. He spent most of his summers traveling to the horse fairs with his father, or riding his dad's mounts in local races and jumping events, or simply for pleasure. He was a bold and fearless rider, and nothing thrilled him more than a free-spirited gallop over the lush, green countryside around Kildorrey.

During the winter months, Mickey rode approximately ten miles to Buttevant where he went to school. The town was a famous horse-trading center, and the site of the first steeplechase hundreds of years earlier. Many days, Mickey never made it to Buttevant or to school, choosing instead, to join local foxhunts he met along the way. When he was discovered, his horse was replaced with a bicycle. To young Mickey, this was a fate worse than death!

In the beautiful countryside and with a family steeped in horsemanship for generations, Mickey lived a horseman's dream, but a boy doesn't often see the treasure that is right before him. Mickey longed for a change from his quiet life, and he ached for adventure. This, he believed, awaited him in the land across the ocean.

One of Mickey's favorite horses in his father's stable was a game and talented gelding named Patrick's Day.

He was fast and strong and Mickey loved to ride him, especially in *flapper races* – local races with few rules. In a flapper race, riders could do anything to win, including shady tactics such as pushing or dragging another rider off his horse, hitting each other with whips, or knocking a competing horse offtrack. A rider had to have a stout heart, a good sense of humor, and a very good, sturdy horse to win these races. Mickey and Patrick's Day were a hard team to beat.

Mickey loved these races, but his dad had other plans for the horse. Mickey and his father eventually had a falling-out over the horse – a disagreement whose details have been lost to time. It was a major row between a boy on the verge of manhood and a father who insisted on continuing to run the show, and it was the push that made Mickey finally decide to head out on his own.

In the spring of 1925, when he was only eighteen years old, a determined Michael G. Walsh boarded a ship that would cross the great Atlantic Ocean, and left his family and Ireland forever.

* * *

That same spring, in a quiet corner of a lush, misty pasture near the great Lough Derg and the River Shannon, a foal was born. His dam, a small, pure-white pony, licked him, nuzzled him, and nickered softly to

her new son. Within half an hour he stood beside her on his wobbly, long legs and drank her rich milk, as the early morning sun and soft breezes dried his dark, wet coat. For that blessed moment he knew only the morning and his gentle mother. He did not know about men or jumps or cheering crowds. But he would.

* * *

Mickey was grinning as he stepped off the ship in New York after a rough ten-day journey. He had been seasick for the first three days, the ship was crowded, and he was wracked with doubts and, at times, fear. He had a sore throat and a cough, but he had made it. He was in America, and he knew in his heart that life would be wonderful from here on in. New York had, just that year, overtaken London as the most populated city in the world, and the Roaring Twenties, a time of great prosperity and high spirits, were at their peak. Money and optimism were flowing freely. Mickey couldn't wait to be a part of it all.

What he didn't know was that more than twenty-seven million immigrants had entered the United States over the past fifty years, about twenty million of them through Ellis Island, a New York processing station established to keep track and control of the enormous flow of people arriving from all over the world. About four million of these immigrants were Irish, and many Americans were becoming unfriendly and unwelcoming toward them. The Irish were often considered to be freeloaders and drunks, even though many thousands of them had gone on to successful and prosperous lives in the new land. Many of the Irish who had arrived in the past came with nothing, simply trying to survive famine and English oppression. They were desperately poor, rural people who had a difficult time adjusting to big city life. It was the image of these unfortunate people that continued to make life difficult for the newer immigrants, like Mickey.

Mickey was surprised at the cold stares, turned backs, harsh words, and signs in the shop windows that read: HIRING. IRISH NEED NOT APPLY. He was surprised, but not discouraged. He had come all the way to America seeking fortune and fame, and he intended to find both. That would prove to be much harder than he could imagine right then.

By that first night, Mickey found a room in a tenement house in an area of Manhattan known as the Bowery. The Bowery had become the place to go for thousands of immigrants who found themselves homeless in New York. It was often a temporary stopover while people settled, found work, and moved to better locations, but it was home for a while. The housing was cheap, offering minimal comforts, and the area was dingy, crowded, and noisy. Crime was abundant, morals were not, and it was fascinating, frightening, and soon, depressing for a boy right off the ship from rural Ireland.

Mickey had enough money to get a start in the city, but it wouldn't last long. He needed to find work quickly. Horses were common in and around New York at that time, but Mickey had left Ireland determined to work at something different. He would not follow in his father's footsteps. There was more to life than the daily chores and lifelong slavery of working with animals. This was his chance to start fresh, find something better, more secure, and profitable.

Two days later, he found ditch digging in Central Park. This was very hard work for a boy as lightly built as Mickey. He had never worked so hard in his life, and he finished each long day so tired and achy that he could barely eat his supper before he fell asleep with rags tied around his blistered hands.

Mickey was soon spending most of his free time in Central Park. It was over eight hundred acres of green space, with carefully developed lakes, bridges, trails, paths, and roadways. There were trees and animals. It was a place to escape and a refuge for someone suffering the first pangs of homesickness. It was the greenest place he could find in the city and he was longing for green. He often saw horses being ridden in the park, and there were days when the sight of them made him long to be back home in Ireland, riding his father's horses as he had for his entire boyhood. Mickey missed the companionship of his family and friends, and the chumminess of the local farmers in the pub. He missed his mother's good meals. Despite himself, more than anything, he missed his father – and the horses.

* * *

The tiny dark colt pressed close to his mother's side and peered at the approaching man with wide, curious eyes. The man was tall with unruly brown hair, large, rough hands, and a long, strong stride. But his brown eyes shone softly, a broad grin spread slowly over his sun-weathered face as he drew nearer, and his voice was deep and gentle when he spoke.

"Ah, Missy, I wasn't expecting this so soon. You are always one to surprise me. What have you got there – a colt this time. A nice little colt, well built. Good for you. Let's get you two into the stable for some breakfast and a closer look." He slipped a halter on the mare's head and led her from the pasture. The foal stayed very close to her side.

In the stable yard, several children came running, squealing with excitement. For a brief moment, the colt wanted to run away. The whites of his eyes showed and he snorted with fear. His mother nickered to him and the man turned to the children. "Quiet down, you'll frighten him," he said, and the children were quiet. As soon as they were in the stall, the colt hid behind his mother, reached for a soothing drink, and peeked from under her belly at all the people staring at him from the stall door.

The man entered, bringing water and grain for the mare. The mare moved eagerly toward the man and her foal quickly understood that this was not someone to fear. When the man put his hand out toward the colt, the colt sniffed it curiously. He did not jump away when the hand moved to stroke his forehead and neck. The hand felt good, petting and rubbing him. The low, rumbling voice was pleasant. It was his first contact with people, and he liked it.

"He's not very big, is he?" said a voice from the stall door.

The man straightened up and glanced toward the door where his oldest son stood. "That's right, Pat, just a little one, this one. I had hoped for a little bigger, crossing her with a thoroughbred and all. That Connemara/

thoroughbred cross is often a good one. The Tetrarch is a fine sire, plenty o' size there. But, it looks like he's taken after his little mam here."

"The Tetrarch's more than just fine. He's one of the grandest racehorses ever born. What is it they called him? The Spotted Wonder? This little guy may grow up bigger and better than we think," said Pat. "Look at the chest on him already, and those straight legs, and barely a day old. He might just turn out to be a nice one."

"Time will tell," answered the man, smiling at his son's enthusiasm. "I think he'll have his mam's good temperament at least. He should make a fine child's hunter if nothing more. Yes, he'll be a nice enough colt for that."

While the talk about his future drifted over him, the colt's head nodded and he folded his legs under him and fell into the deep, pleasant sleep of the very young.

In the following weeks, the colt became the pet of the stable. He soon had no fear of people, large or small, and he enjoyed all of the attention he received on his daily visits to the stable. The children stroked and scratched him and the man led him around with a halter until he was quite used to how it worked. He was handled all over until he would tolerate being touched in even the most ticklish spots. He was taught to lift his feet and stand as the man rubbed and tapped on his hooves. This would help later on when he needed his hooves trimmed or shod.

Several other foals were born in the weeks that followed and the colt spent his days in the broodmare pasture, running, playing, sleeping, drinking, and running again with his companions. It was a very pleasant start to his life.

2

Difficult Beginnings

*M*ickey was soon following the horses back to their stables and hanging around the arenas where riders worked their mounts over small jump courses or on the flat. The young man was a sorry sight. His clothes had become worn and dirty. Hard work, scanty meals, and the sore throat that still plagued him had left him thinner than when he had first left Ireland's shores. He wasn't a tall boy, and in his present condition, he looked younger than his eighteen years. He was tired and lonely and longing for a change, but his eyes shone brightly at the sight of the horses. His grin was quick and inviting and he spoke eagerly to anyone who was within range. Mickey Walsh hadn't given up.

One evening, he watched as a man struggled with a headstrong, young mare, trying to make her flex into a small, right-hand circle. The horse resisted, pulling her head to the left, stiffening her neck, and bolting as the man became more insistent. The man was becoming frustrated and the horse steadily more upset and balky. Mickey overheard someone commenting on the rider's skill as they walked by.

"That's a tough horse. He'll work it out, though. He's one of the best trainers around here."

Mickey frowned and thought, *If this is what they consider great in America, I could do well here. They could use a few lessons in Irish horsemanship!* Mickey had never offered advice to any of the riders before, but now could not stay quiet.

"Ease up on the left rein and open your circle a bit," he called out.

The rider stopped the horse and looked at Mickey through narrowed eyes. His cheeks were red from exertion and frustration. "What?" he snapped.

"You're holding your left rein too rigid and she's obviously not ready for such a small circle," said Mickey.

"Open it up and let her relax into it, then close it back up gradually once she's flexed."

For a moment the man looked annoyed. He stared at Mickey, sizing him up, then suddenly, his face relaxed into a smile. "You think you know more than me, do you?" It was said pleasantly, not as a challenge.

Mickey grinned and said, "I know more than most when it comes to horses, sir. I've been riding them since I was born, same as my dad and granddad. I could get your filly to bend for you."

The man raised his eyebrows at the suggestion, then shrugged and smiled again. He dismounted and held out the reins to Mickey. "She's not easy to ride. I hope you know as much as you say, or you'll be on your back in the dust in a moment."

A surge of excitement coursed through Mickey's body. He'd been longing to ride for days. He mounted lightly and thrilled at the feel of the filly's muscles as she jumped forward, startled by the new, lighter weight on her back. He felt her mouth through the reins and began to communicate to her gently with his hands, legs, and voice. He rode her around the arena until she stopped shying and began to relax and respond to his quiet requests. Ten minutes later, Mickey rode her in a small, right-hand circle, perfectly flexed and relaxed.

He pulled her up before the man, dismounted, and bowed dramatically.

The man laughed out loud, impressed. "What's your name?"

"Mickey Walsh."

"Well, Mickey Walsh, you've got some talent there. I've seldom seen such fine and sensitive riding. I have some friends in New Jersey who are always looking for stablehands and riders. Any chance you might be interested?"

Mickey nodded without hesitation, his good-natured grin wider than ever. It went against his plan, but after only a week of digging ditches, he knew for certain that he didn't want to do that any longer. He'd work with horses just for a while, until he found something else, something better. For the first time since he had arrived, Mickey returned to his boarding house whistling and with a spring in his stride. He was heading for New Jersey and the beginning of better times.

The job in New Jersey would not last long, however. By the time Mickey settled in a week later, he was ill. His joints were painful, he was feverish, and he could not hold down any food. He tried to ignore it, determined to keep the job, but his body was sapped of strength and energy, and he had a difficult time with the work. He had

rheumatic fever – a result of the untreated strep infection he had picked up on the ship. Mickey tried to keep up, waking early to work the pain out of his joints, forcing himself to eat food when he didn't feel like it. In spite of his efforts, he became steadily weaker and was soon let go.

He headed back to the Bowery and Central Park, where he spent weeks resting and recovering. He was weak and thin and very tired, but the playful grin that would one day become so well known and loved, was still quick to light up his face. It won him the aid of new friends, including an Irish "cop" who patrolled Central Park on horseback.

With this man's help, Mickey soon found himself on Long Island, mucking stalls at the private stable of Mr. George Melbourne. The young Irish lad had not yet regained his full strength, but he could keep up with the work. He'd had a rough start, but things were finally starting to look up.

*   *   *

The colt was shedding his dark coat as he approached his first birthday and he was now a gray – not white like his dam – but much lighter than he had been. He spent less time with his mother now, preferring the company of the other frisky yearlings who wanted to run and play as much as he did. Besides, the mare was heavy with a new foal now, and she was not moving quickly.

One warm, spring morning, the man led him away from the stable without the mare. The colt wasn't concerned at first, as he often went without his mother for short periods of time. But then, instead of going straight ahead to the broodmare pasture, the man led his yearling to the right and down a long lane. The colt stopped and jerked back on the lead, suddenly frightened. The man rubbed the youngster's neck and soothed him.

"It's all right, Little One. Nothing to worry about. Your mam needs all her energy to get ready for a new baby, now. It's time for you young ones to go on your own." He coaxed the colt forward and they came to the gate of a large, rolling pasture. Three other yearlings were already there. Two of them grazed restlessly, stopping every few seconds to lift their heads and listen alertly. The third paced a stretch of fence, whinnying frantically for her mother. The man slipped the halter off the colt's head and turned him loose in the new pasture. By the end of the hour, seven unhappy yearlings had been brought there to start a new phase of their lives.

The colt didn't like it. He joined the filly at the fence, running back and forth and snorting with frustration.

He was too far from the stable, from the people and activity, and from his mother. He was much smaller than the other yearlings. He had to crane his neck to see over the great stone wall that surrounded this new field. He was angry and frightened for the first time in his life. He did not want to be in this strange place.

He began running out, away from the fence, and then charging straight at it. Each time he stopped at the very last second, body bunched and ready to spring. The solid stone fence was a formidable barrier. It was unlikely that even the taller yearlings could jump it successfully, and an unsuccessful jump could be fatal. Yet, on the fourth charge, he leaped and sailed over the stones, clearing them easily. He landed on the other side and stopped, surprised. Then, with a whinny, he trotted up the lane to the broodmare pasture.

"How in the world did you get out of that field!" exclaimed the man.

He caught the colt, led him back to the yearling pasture, and turned him loose again. This time he stayed to watch.

With no hesitation, the colt galloped to the center of the field, turned and charged toward the fence, sailed over it, and trotted triumphantly back to his mother's pasture.

"Well, I'll be darned!" exclaimed the astonished man. "We've got ourselves a jumper. He cleared that fence on the first attempt!"

The colt spent the rest of that week in a high-walled arena. In a few days he stopped pacing and screaming and grew sulky. He was bored and lonely and he did not so much as nicker when the man came in to visit him on the fifth morning of his confinement.

"So, shall we try again, lad?" asked the man in his rich, deep voice as he slipped a halter over the small gray head. "Let's get you back with your mates and no more silliness now. Save your big jumps for the show ring. You've earned yourself a show name and everything now, did you know that? First Attempt is what we'll call you. How does that sound?"

The man turned him loose. First Attempt hesitated, trotted to the fence, looking toward his mother's pasture and the stable. Then he turned away, lured by the smell of the fresh green grass and the sight of his stablemates at the far end of the field. He snatched a bite of the sweet grass and headed off at a trot. The man sighed with relief.

First Attempt spent the next two years in that big pasture with the other young horses, living the easiest of lives. A small, dense wood at the far end of the pasture afforded shelter from the frequent rain and occasional hot sun. The Slieve Aughty Mountains rose to the west, and from the highest point in the field, a sliver of shimmering blue could be seen – the Lough Derg, one of Ireland's largest lakes.

Occasionally, First Attempt was taken to the stable where his hooves would be trimmed, and he would be groomed and handled a bit, but most of the time he and the herd were left alone to eat and play and grow.

By his third spring, the colt's coat had lightened to pale silver. In time, he would be as white as his mother. He had developed nicely, with a fine head, a long, arched neck, and straight legs. His chest was wide and his haunches powerful. Still, the other horses towered over him. They were all long-legged thoroughbreds or thoroughbred crosses, like him. But, when he was measured that spring, he was only thirteen hands high, or fifty-two inches. Everyone agreed that a child's pony was all he would amount to. Yet, the man remembered the mighty jump that was the colt's namesake and he saw, every day, a special spirit in the eyes of this pony, and secretly wondered if something greater might be in store for him.

3

Rising Stars

*M*ickey had been working on the Melbourne Estate on Long Island for well over a year when he received a letter that would change the course of his life. He had quickly won the respect and affection of the Melbourne family and was now well established within the horse community. He was training and showing the Melbourne's small string of horses, as well as giving lessons and schooling clients' horses. He was twenty years old and well liked for his sense of humor, light-hearted nature, and his obvious skill as a horseman. Mickey was still treating this as a temporary job, but others saw a talent and passion that told them otherwise.

Mickey grinned when he read the return address on the envelope. Kitty Roche, an old school chum from Ireland, recently arrived on Long Island. Kitty from Shamballymore and "more if you want it." Kitty from "the bog," riding a donkey to school. How he had teased her. He tore open the letter and read the short note eagerly:

I arrived this spring with my brother, Jack, and after a short time in the Bowery (not short enough!), I found work as a cleaning lady, opening the estates of owners who winter in Manhattan and summer on Long Island. Can you believe how rich these people are? These places are mansions and the grounds are so enormous and immaculate.

I've worked in a couple of different places and I'm now second cook (I cook for the staff, but not the owners) for a Swedish family. I am the only English-speaking girl here. I am very lonely and longing for home . . .

Mickey went to her right away and was pleasantly surprised to find that the girl he had left almost two years ago had blossomed into a very lovely young woman of seventeen. He had forgotten how blue her eyes were. Had he ever even noticed? And the soft auburn waves of her hair tempted him to touch them. He had never felt like that before.

Mickey arranged for Kitty to move to the Melbourne Estate and work there as second cook. From that time on, they were never apart. They were married within the year and Mickey could not have found a more loyal, warm, and loving partner.

Mickey and Kitty remained with the Melbournes until 1929, when two major events brought change to their lives once more. First, the Great Depression began, following the sudden crash of the stock market on October 29, a day that would always be remembered as Black Tuesday. Great numbers of wealthy people instantly lost everything. It was the beginning of a desperate time, not only in New York, but around the world, and unskilled immigrants would suffer greatly.

The second event, a happier one, was the birth of Mickey and Kitty's first child, a boy they named Thomas, after Mickey's father.

The Melbournes were no longer able to employ Mickey or Kitty, and for the next few years, they went wherever work could be found. Luckily, Mickey's skill with horses had become well known and finding work was somewhat easier for him than for many others. These were hard, lean years, and though it wasn't always easy, Mickey was able to keep food on his family's table and a roof over their heads.

First, he worked at a riding stable near Lake Ronkonkoma, Long Island, and then at a second stable at Russell Gardens, New York. After that, he found work with another great Irish horseman, Jim Rice, at his farm at Great Neck, Long Island. This was a turning point in Mickey's career. Jim Rice and Mickey Walsh formed a splendid partnership. The two men were well matched in both skill and humor, and on Jim's horses, Mickey rose steadily higher in the show world. He began, at last, to see that horses were his life, and always would be.

During the Walsh family's time at Rice Farm, a second child, Kathleen, was born – and an old rift was mended between father and son.

Jim, who had also been a horse trader in Ireland, often discussed with Mickey how grand the Irish horses were, and how the Americans could use some "good Irish blood" to improve the quality of their horses.

"My dad's an impeccable judge of horses – he can see ability and heart in an animal better than anyone I've ever known," Mickey told Jim proudly. "Why don't we have him pick you out a good horse for your stable and ship it over?" Jim agreed, a price was set, and Mickey wrote to his father, describing what Mr. Rice was looking for and asking for his help.

The letter was more than a business proposal. It was a mature gesture of forgiveness and understanding. It was well received.

After a lengthy process, the horse was finally found and shipped to New York City Harbor, and then sent by train to Long Island, where Mickey was waiting for it. He was anxious and eager to please Jim Rice, but when the horse stepped off the train, his heart sank. It was a mare – he had been expecting a stallion. She'd had a rough trip and was thin and ragged – nothing like what he had expected.

He rode the mare home that night, a journey of about fifteen miles. Along the way, he tested her gaits, jumped anything he could find to jump, and got to know her very quickly. By the time they reached the stable, Mickey was convinced his father had found the perfect horse that met all their expectations. She was bold and strong and well balanced. She refused nothing, and despite her weariness and poor physical state, she showed heart. Jim Rice was not disappointed and the brood mare became one of the central horses in his stable.

This was the first of many similar transactions

and the beginning of a renewed relationship of trust and respect between Mickey and his father. The rift that had torn them apart and nearly driven Mickey away from a career in horses was ended. Although times were hard, Mickey's life was full and happy. He felt as though the world were in his hands.

Then, in 1931, tragedy struck. Two-year-old Thomas was playing near a lake. Somehow, the robust toddler fell, striking his head. Before help could reach him, Thomas had drowned. For a time, it seemed that life would never be happy for Mickey again. He blamed himself, and the death of his young son crushed him as nothing ever had before. What solace he could find was in the horses. With them he was able to concentrate on the rides and stop thinking about Thomas for short spells, as he focused on the animals beneath him.

In his pain, Mickey rode better than ever, and caught the attention of a woman named Audrey Kennedy. Audrey owned a high-ranking hunter/jumper stable in Massachusetts, and she invited Mickey to work as her private trainer and show rider. Mickey accepted. The shattered family moved to Audwill Stables near the end of 1931, and there they would remain, healing, growing, and changing, for nearly twenty years.

* * *

First Attempt went into training near the end of his third summer. He was a high-spirited colt, but he had his dam's sensible nature and love of people, and he took to the saddle and bridle without much difficulty. Because of his size, the children were his first riders. They were accomplished equestrians and his training was carried out under the watchful eye of their father. The even-tempered colt never knew a rough hand and he was brought along slowly and carefully, and given time to learn each lesson thoroughly before being asked to do more.

One of the man's sons took a special interest in him, and began to ride him in the local shows in flat classes (no jumps). First Attempt was "green" and he could be a handful at times, but he took to the hustle and bustle of the show grounds and seemed to enjoy the attention and activity. The family soon decided to introduce him to jumping.

First Attempt was a born jumper. He took to it naturally and cleared obstacles as though he had springs in his legs. Over the next two years he competed in increasingly difficult competitions, and he did well. He had reached his full height now – a mere thirteen point two hands – but he soon proved that he could hold his own, even in open competition against full-sized horses. He was no ordinary pony.

This was apparent to Captain Daniel Corry of the Irish Free State Army Equestrian Team, who began to follow the developing career of the little gray pony with interest. Dan Corry kept a private string of show horses at a farm in Galway and was always on the lookout for good horses to add to his string or to train for resale.

One morning in 1930, at a show in Dublin, he watched First Attempt win a basic dressage class and admired the pony's free and powerful action. Later, in a jumping competition, he found himself caught up with the crowd as First Attempt cleared impressive jumps with a flash and grace that made it seem effortless.

Captain Corry offered to buy First Attempt that afternoon, and after some haggling, the deal was done. First Attempt would never see his home again.

Captain Corry, a small, lightly built man, loved the spunky pony, and brought him along over the next two years until he was a polished performer and a very successful one. In 1932, First Attempt became Champion Jumper at the Dublin Horse Show when he cleared six-foot-six to win the Stonewall Jumping class.

A few weeks later he was boarding a ship that would take him to America. Captain Corry was accompanying the Irish Free State Army team on a tour of international competitions and he had decided to take First Attempt along. First Attempt was now seven years old, pure white, and up for sale.

Captain Corry entered First Attempt in several shows during their trip and at the Boston Garden Show they caught the attention of a fourteen-year-old boy called Fred Tolman, who promptly talked his father into buying First Attempt for him to use as a hunter/jumper. Harry Tolman, also impressed by the pony's style and ability, was easily persuaded. The price was rather high for the time, but you couldn't buy one of the famous Irish ponies for nothing, and Fred was so eager and persistent that the deal was soon settled.

At the Tolman farm, it soon became evident that First Attempt was not a quiet and gentle child's pony, but a well-trained performance horse. He was well-mannered and loved to please, but he was fit and full of life and his sire's thoroughbred spirit came through in him. Young Fred became frustrated with him when he pranced and shied and, just for fun, threw in an occasional buck. First Attempt soon realized that the boy was not as skilled or confident as his previous riders had been, and began to take advantage of him. First Attempt was a strong, clever pony and Fred was not his match.

The novelty of owning the beautiful white pony and the dreams of being the star of the hunter/jumper classes soon faded, and First Attempt spent most of the next two years growing soft in the Tolman's pasture. He was used only occasionally by his nervous young owner, attending the occasional competition around New England, and it looked as though his successful rise in the show world was ended. This might have been the case had he not caught the attention of Danny Shea while performing at a small show.

Danny Shea, a well-known and respected horseman, had an eye for a good horse. He liked what he saw in First Attempt – the angle of shoulder and fetlock, the width of chest, powerful hindquarters, straight legs, and fine head. It all went together to create a smooth, floating trot, an even canter, and enormous power over the jumps. But more importantly, Danny saw the pony try his best every time, saw the spirited way First Attempt moved, and the playfulness he exhibited, even under the stress of a less than suitable rider. The pony had heart – an indescribable quality that great athletes in all sports possess. Danny saw all this and knew the pony could be much better than he was.

Danny purchased First Attempt in 1935. The pony was ten years old – in his prime, sound, well trained, and ready to move into major competition. Danny's thirteen-year-old son, Danny Jr., was a light, sensitive, successful rider, and a rising star in the show world. He was perfectly suited for First Attempt and eager to ride for his father.

Danny Sr. had recently sold a large gray gelding named Squire to the Canadian Army Equestrian Team. Squire was a champion jumper and the senior Shea's favorite. Everyone agreed that First Attempt looked like a smaller version of Squire and had a similar spunky, but friendly attitude. Danny decided to change the pony's name to Little Squire in honor of his old mount. With his new name and under his new rider, the talented pony flourished.

For the next three years, Little Squire and Danny Shea Jr. showed the New York jumping world what they were all about. Danny Jr. was a very capable young horseman and was steadily climbing the ranks in competition. Little Squire gave his all in whatever classes Danny entered him, and together, they took home many first-place ribbons and several championships. It seemed that Little Squire was at his best with Danny Jr. Surprisingly, though, he would get even better.

4

Little Squire and Mickey Together

Oddly enough, it was not one of these spectacular performances of boy and pony that brought Little Squire to Mickey's attention. Danny Shea Sr. and Mickey Walsh often competed at the same events and knew each other well. Mickey was now considered one of the most talented professional show riders of his time, and he frequently coached Danny Jr. at the shows and in private. Mickey, of course, already knew about Little Squire and, like everyone who had witnessed him jump, was very impressed by the pony.

It was at the Cohasset show on Long Island, where Mickey saw something in the pony that really made him interested. Danny Shea's younger son, Bobby, now about thirteen or fourteen years old, was riding Little Squire in a jumping class. He was good, but inexperienced, and not as naturally talented as his brother, Danny, had been at that age. The jumps were moderate, just under four feet high, but the course was fairly difficult, with several tight turns and a tricky combination near the end.

Bobby was in trouble from the start. He started with the wrong jump, and from there was forced to jump the course backward. This was dangerous. If a rail was hit, it would not come down as it would if hit from the correct side. A hit rail could mean a bad trip for the horse, possibly causing him to flip. One mistake could mean a serious accident.

Bobby realized his mistake within the first couple of jumps, and by the time they reached the combination, his riding had become somewhat erratic, as though he kept changing his mind as he tried to decide what to do. He appeared to pull Little Squire up and everyone thought he was withdrawing from the class. But then he leaned forward and pushed Little Squire, once more, toward the rails.

With only moments to regain his stride and no time

to properly gain momentum for the difficult series of jumps, it didn't look good for Little Squire. Danny and Mickey held their breath as the game little pony shook his head and grabbed for the bit. Bobby settled quietly in the saddle, resigned to let Little Squire handle the rest.

Little Squire cleared the combination and the rest of the course cleanly and left the ring to a collective sigh of relief from all who were watching. Mickey was unusually quiet as he followed Danny and a shaken Bobby back to the stabling area. Mickey didn't hear the words exchanged between father and son, and hardly noticed as they removed the saddle from Little Squire's back. Mickey was in Ireland, chasing foxes on his sturdy little school pony, riding home from a distant fair on a rank horse his father had just purchased, galloping Patrick's Day across green fields. . . .

He turned suddenly to Danny. "Where did you say you got this pony?"

Danny saw something in Mickey's face then, an intensity and excitement he had come to recognize well. Mickey had noticed it – the special something that went beyond talent, beyond a well-built horse. He had watched Little Squire take control, negotiate the course when his young rider could not, keep them both safe with his skill and courage.

Mickey already knew much of Little Squire's history, but he didn't know everything. Danny grinned and went to the tack trunk, where he pulled out a ratty-looking scrapbook full of photos, ribbons, and articles. When he returned, he was holding out a newspaper article for Mickey to read.

No animal in the show ring today has a stranger background than the extraordinary jumping pony, Little Squire. His story, as told by Captain Corry and endorsed by Captain Fred Aherne, is as follows:

"First Attempt, as he was called in those days, is by The Tetrarch, out of a little Connemara pony mare, and was bred and raised by the King of the Fairies in Ireland. For some time the king hunted him in the Tipperary country, and so great a name did he make for himself there, that His Majesty decided to take him up to a hunt with the fashionable Meath pack and show all the fine ladies and gentlemen there how to go. But, on his very first outing with Meath, the little pony jumped so big and strong over one of those terrible drains that the poor king, God rest his soul, fell off and broke his neck. And that's how Captain Corry came to own

*the pony, because the king would never have parted
with him otherwise."*

Mickey, with his keen sense of humor and fondness for
Ireland, loved the story and was very taken with the
pony. His talent was obvious enough, but any creature
with such a story attached to it must be something
extra special.

That evening, he spoke to Audrey Kennedy about
buying the pony to add to her string. Audrey had come
to trust Mickey entirely where the horses were concerned. He had taken her stable to new heights and she
had never met a more intuitive horseman. But now,
she wondered if he had lost his edge.

"What, that little pony?" she exclaimed.

"Yes. He's quite wonderful. He'd be great for us."

"He's so tiny. Our level of competition would kill
him."

"He's already proven that he can do it. He may be
small, but he jumps like a full-sized horse."

Mickey recounted the stats for her – the six-foot-six
Stone Wall win, the numerous wins over four-foot
jumps and, recently, some very impressive wins over
five-foot jumps with young Danny Shea.

"And you've seen him," he added. "There's just

something special about him. Think about it, Audrey. You won't regret it."

In the end, it was Audrey's husband, William, who talked her into it. He, too, had taken a fancy to the gutsy little pony, and longed to see what he could do in Mickey's capable hands. Audrey agreed reluctantly, and in the spring of 1938, she purchased the pony for fifteen hundred dollars (a lot of money at that time). Little Squire made the journey to Gibbs Island, Massachusetts to join the Audwill Stable's string of stars, including Audrey's favorite, Erin's Son.

If Mickey had any doubts about talking Audrey into buying the pony, they disappeared the moment he first rode Little Squire. Little Squire was quick, responsive, and light in Mickey's hands. His gaits were smooth and he was very well trained. But there was something else, something Mickey could not put into words. Little Squire actually seemed to enjoy working. He put a spark into it that made even a simple, flat exercise exciting. Mickey could feel the energy tingle through Little Squire when he was put to the jumps. The pony loved to jump – and he was good at it.

At some point during that first ride, Mickey connected with Little Squire in a way that no rider had connected with the pony before. Mickey knew with absolute certainty that he was riding one of the best horses he had ever ridden.

Audrey entered Little Squire in his first competition two weeks later. It was a small show in Albany, New York, but the field was challenging. Although it was still only June, horses and riders were competing in earnest, their sights set on the National Horse Show at Madison Square Gardens, scheduled in November. This was the most important U.S. equestrian event at the time, drawing top-notch national horses and international teams. Only the best would go, and the best were proven at these smaller shows.

The Kennedys had a strong string of contenders that year, and hoped to be one of the major forces on the hunter/jumper scene. Whether Little Squire could keep up at that level, was yet to be seen. He began to answer that question in Albany, leaving the two-day event with the championship.

Two weeks later, he earned the Open Jumper Championship at the Westchester Country Club Horse Show, in Rye, New York, placing first in the Daily Open Stakes and the Four-Foot Class, and second in the Touch and Go Stakes, where speed and dexterity were essential. That day, he was a full two hands (eight inches) smaller than any rival horse in the competition. The crowds loved him and the bond between Mickey and the pony grew stronger with every ride.

At home, Little Squire had become Mickey's pet. Mickey spent hours with him, grooming him, playing with him, and teaching the eldest of his five children to ride him. Little Squire responded with unfaltering loyalty and affection, following Mickey around like a puppy, sometimes going right up to the front door when Mickey went in for a meal. Mickey's children loved him, especially his daughter, Kathleen. At seven, she was like her dad, a fearless, skilled rider, and she could handle the feisty performer very well. Little Squire received the best of care, and the bond he shared with Mickey was something rare and remarkable to witness.

Little Squire walked away with championships in his next two shows. People really began to take notice of this unstoppable pony. As the build-up to the Nationals continued, it became apparent that Little Squire would not only earn his place in the competition, but he might just be the one to beat.

Through September he improved, growing stronger with each competition. At the Boston Fair in mid-September, Little Squire earned his seventh championship. He had been entered in seven shows since becoming a part of the Audwill string.

William Kennedy was excited, bragging to reporters that he had had to beg Danny Shea to sell the pony, and how happy the Kennedys were that he had. Little Squire had won more ribbons in his three months with them than he had for any other rider in the past four years. The media was delighted. They played up the rivalry between William's favorite, Little Squire, and Audrey's favorite, Erin's Son, who had also been performing very well that summer.

Little Squire was now considered one of the leading show-jumpers in the east, and better yet, he was a crowd thriller. He loved an audience, pricking his ears expectantly after every performance, arching his neck and prancing at the expected applause. He seemed to have a genuine sense of humor, which made him the perfect match for Mickey, who also enjoyed showing off. Besides putting on brilliant performances, the pair would often play to the crowds, pleasing them – and the media – even more. As a team, Mickey and Little Squire were the ideal blend of talent, passion, and playfulness. Mickey was convinced that Little Squire could do it all.

Could Little Squire keep up the pace? Even dynamite ponies have their limits. The competitions were getting tougher and tougher, leading up to the Nationals. The jumps were higher, the courses more difficult, the horses better – and bigger.

At the prestigious Boston Horse Show, the final major event before Madison Square Gardens, Little Squire faltered. Mickey noticed that he seemed "off" during a warm-up the first day of the show. He wasn't lame and he was eating well. There was nothing obvious, but something was different.

The stands were filled with fans who had come to watch "the littlest horse with the biggest heart" (as he was now dubbed by the press), beat the pants off the bigger horses. They were disappointed, watching instead, as the pony struggled with the higher jumps and left the arena defeated, time and again.

Although Mickey was not a big man, he suddenly looked far too large for the pony. The effort required for Little Squire to carry him over five-foot fences was comparable to a bigger horse carrying a two-hundred-pound man over eight-foot jumps. For the first time since coming to Audwill Stables, he was not the champion at the end of the four-day show. And for the first time, there was doubt as to whether he could go all the way.

Mickey was concerned, and went over him with a fine-toothed comb. The vet could find nothing wrong

– no soreness in his legs or back, no fever, nothing unusual in his blood or urine tests. He just didn't have his usual kick, and he was quiet. The vet suggested that he might have a mild virus, or perhaps he was simply tired and needed a break. He had turned fourteen years old, after all.

Mickey turned Little Squire out to pasture for a week, and then slowly brought him back into light training, allowing only little Kathleen to ride him. Then, about ten days before the Nationals, Little Squire squealed and gave a mighty buck during his morning workout, sending young Kathleen head over heels. Before Mickey could reach her, Little Squire had turned around and trotted back to her, nickering and nuzzling her as she sat up. Kathleen was unhurt, and they both seemed surprised that she had come off. Mickey laughed and laughed. It seemed the old spark had returned. Mickey didn't ride him until just days before they were to leave for the show, but he knew right away that the old Squire was back. The energy was there, and the pony tossed his head and pranced, very pleased to have his proper rider again.

5

The National Horse Show

Saturday, November 4, 1939 – the opening day of the National Horse Show. Newspapers throughout New York heralded the tales of glamor and excitement that unfolded during the week, happy to have something to lift people's spirits and distract them from the overseas events of World War II.

The show would run for seven days, featuring more than two thousand horses in over a hundred classes, from gaited horses to harness horses, from dressage demonstrations to children's pony events. The highlights, though, were the hunter and jumper competitions, and these drew crowds from every level of New York society.

But the show organizers had reason to be concerned. The war was having a major effect on the events. By the eve of its opening, pathetically few international jumping teams had entered. The excitement and patriotism that the Irish, Canadian, English, and Continental army teams had always inspired, was to be missing this year.

Amazingly, the show was far from a failure. Enthusiasm remained high, and ticket sales strong. Against all odds, the entire week was a remarkable success, and part of that success came in the form of a little white pony who had stolen hearts across the nation.

Audwill Stables, with its strong contingent of horses, was creating quite a stir. Somehow the press caught wind of a rumor that the Kennedys might have young Kathleen ride Little Squire in his classes, instead of Mickey. The Kennedys neither confirmed nor denied this, leaving fans and competitors in suspense over what would happen during the show. In fact, having Kathleen ride was never a consideration. Little Squire was in top form, and Mickey was ready to have fun.

For the next six days, thousands of people thronged to Madison Square Gardens, hoping to be thrilled once more by the spectacular little white jumping pony. This time, there was no disappointment. The classes were large, with twenty to thirty horses entered in each. Competition was fierce and the courses were very tough. One special course was so difficult, it raised a fair amount of criticism from competitors and spectators alike. Many complained that most of the horses couldn't manage it, but it didn't stop Little Squire.

Little Squire opened the jumping events with his first win in the Pen Jump. On day two, he "set the house on fire" with a second, utterly spectacular win, out-jumping twenty-seven rivals in the Touch and Out Class over the Special Course. Every newspaper in the city carried the story.

In The Rocket, he jumped a clean round of four-foot jumps, but had a knock-down during the five-foot round, ending up second to a big horse called Watch Me. In every class he entered, Little Squire sent the crowd wild, and he and Mickey became more and more animated. Before one class, they jumped into the orchestra pit, turned around, and leaped back out, a feat impossible for a larger horse. Before another class, Mickey walked Little Squire under one of the formidable jumps, turned him around, and jumped it. The crowd roared.

They were a little too exuberant for the Handy Class, where horses are judged on both performance and manners. Little Squire jumped the difficult course well, but became a bit strong near the end, causing him to knock down two rails in a tough, three-jump combination. Mickey laughed as he accepted the third-place ribbon.

By the final night, Little Squire was leading the standings with fourteen points. Mickey had only to guide him to second place in the Jumper Stakes to earn the championship. Little Squire had no difficulty jumping the first round clean, while most of the other entries were eliminated. The jump-off came down to four horses, including Little Squire and an enormous, sixteen-point-two hand gelding named Catch Me. In the jump-off, the horses had to perform not only clean, but fast. The course was shorter, but more difficult. The fastest time with the fewest knock-downs would win.

The first two horses went quickly, but each suffered knock-downs. Catch Me was not quite as quick, but he jumped clean. If Little Squire could jump clean, just a fraction faster, he'd be first. As long as he was faster and had no more than one knock-down, he'd be second in the class and the Open Jumper Champion of the show. Mickey rode to win both the class and the championship.

The gallery cheered as Little Squire entered the ring, and screamed with every jump he cleared. Little Squire flew around the course, jumping the great fences with tremendous power and by the third-last jump, the crowd was on its feet, urging him on. A collective groan rose from the crowd when Little Squire brushed the second last fence. The pole wobbled, then came down as Little Squire cleared the final fence. As Little Squire trotted to the exit, the crowd gave him a standing ovation, despite his loss, for he had earned the Open Jumper Championship, and their hearts.

Two hours later, Little Squire entered the ring to the whistles and cheers of a crowd once more on its feet. He had earned a total of twenty-one points, ten ahead of the Reserve Champion, Port Light, who finished the week with eleven points. Mickey grinned proudly as the championship ribbon was attached to Little Squire's bridle, then Mickey Walsh did something nobody expected and nobody would soon forget. He turned the pony loose, walked out of the ring, and closed the five-foot gate behind him. For a moment, Little Squire surveyed the stands, as though sizing up the crowd. They watched him, puzzled and hushed. Then, with a squeal, Little Squire spun and galloped to the gate, leaped over it, and trotted to Mickey, who stood waiting on the other side. People went wild with delight. Applause and laughter followed Mickey and Little Squire as they headed down the ramp, to the stable area below.

An article in the *New York Herald Tribune* on Sunday, November 12, 1939, described Little Squire's victory:

14,000 Attend Horse Show's Brilliant End – Little Squire Wins Jumper's Title

A closing night audience, lush in furs and glittering with sequins, saw the most fabulous open jumper in American horse-show history win the Jumper Championship of the fifty-fourth annual National Horse Show at Madison Square Gardens.

Little Squire was at the top. He had won championships in all but one show in the past six months – a record never before equaled in that level of show jumping. He was the Open Jumper Champion at the most prestigious event in the United States, beating the best – and biggest – at their game, and he was a crowd pleaser. He seemed unstoppable.

6

Life at the Top

*L*ittle Squire and the other Kennedy horses were moved to Jacob's Hill for the winter to rest, but by April, they were back in the show ring.

Little Squire had worked hard for most of his life. Could such a small, aging pony put in another season at such a strenuous pace? Mickey thought so. Every day, as he handled and rode Little Squire, he felt that familiar surge of energy that told him the pony was still in top form. Mickey would know when Squire had had enough.

One afternoon, in Southern Pines, North Carolina,

after a show where they had earned yet another championship ribbon, Mickey and some other horsemen leaned on a paddock rail, watching Little Squire relax in the evening sun.

"It's incredible the way that pony can jump," said one of the men.

"He's a hellava leaper. I believe he could jump anything," answered Mickey.

"Every horse has its limit," said another man.

"Not Little Squire," said Mickey. "He'd jump over six feet with me riding bareback, if I asked him to."

"Get out of here. That's impossible," said the first man. "I mean, without a rider maybe. But with you bareback, clinging up top? No way."

"Little Squire could do it," answered Mickey confidently.

"Not a chance, though I'd like to see you try. I'll bet you fifty dollars that he can't do it."

"I'll bet you a hundred that he can," Mickey said.

"A hundred! You're on."

Soon, the arrangements were made. A difficult, straight-rail jump was set up at six-foot-two, and a cameraman was arranged to capture the moment – for good or bad. Word had spread around the stable and every groom, trainer, and stablehand was there to watch.

More then a few bets were made between those present.

Little Squire was brought into the arena, wearing only a bridle.

"You said no tack," called out the man with whom Mickey had made his wager.

"I said bareback, but we can go without the bridle, too," said Mickey casually. "I'll just keep it on to warm him up."

"He's crazy," said one of the spectators. "He's going to kill himself, or that pony. This is impossible."

Mickey spoke to Little Squire as they trotted around the arena, warming up. What he said to him, nobody knows, but whatever it was worked. A few minutes later, Mickey slipped the bridle off Little Squire's head, and guided him once more around the arena to face the mighty jump. Mickey urged Little Squire into a gallop then let the pony do the rest. Little Squire ran straight at the jump and gave a mighty leap, clearing the rail with room to spare. Mickey barely moved on his back, and on the landing, he slid off the pony and hugged him, laughing. The resulting photo became as famous as the playful pair, and was reproduced many times over the years.

Spring blended into summer in a blur of shows, ribbons, and applause. Little Squire was in fine form, and continued to steal championship honors away from the larger horses.

In July 1940, Little Squire thrilled crowds once again at the Huntington Horse Show on Long Island, in an event that was making a revival after a ten-year lapse. It was the High Jump, and it turned out to be the climax of the show.

Two horses had been in the limelight throughout the two-day competition. Little Squire, who'd been ridden the entire show by Mickey's daughter, Kathleen, and My Play Boy, a fifteen-hand bay, ridden by thirteen-year-old Russell Stewart. The two young equestrians had been racing for the championship neck and neck, beating out mature riders on bigger, capable horses. Ironically, Mickey, aboard Erin's Son, was one of them. It was during the High Jump where the two little horses really put on a show.

The initial jump was set at five feet – a schooling jump. The crowd was uneasy when Kathleen rode in, hardly daring to believe that she might be able to ride the entire, dangerous class. Four other horses were entered, including My Play Boy, Erin's Son, and two other big horses named The Scoundrel and Beer Baron.

The Scoundrel was out in the first round at five feet. Everyone else, including Little Squire and Kathleen, jumped clean. The bar was raised to five-foot-six. Beer Baron and Erin's Son were both eliminated at this height, leaving the two smallest horses and the two youngest riders to finish.

An uncomfortable murmur went through the stands as the bar was raised to five-foot-nine. Surely Kathleen, as good a rider as she was, could not be expected to guide the pony safely over that height. A cheer went up when Little Squire entered the arena with Mickey aboard. But could Little Squire do it now? He was six inches shorter than My Play Boy and he was now under double the weight he had been carrying during the first two rounds.

Each horse was allowed three attempts. Little Squire was the first to go. The pole came down on the first two tries and the crowd was hushed. The weight was too much, the height too much, and he was tiring. His chances were not looking good.

Mickey gave him a loose rein and walked him slowly around the arena, letting him catch his breath and relax before the third try. Mickey walked him close to the jump, accentuating the height, building the crowd, rubbing in the effect. He knew Little Squire could do this, but it was always more fun if people thought he couldn't. When Mickey took up his reins at last, and

Little Squire broke into a trot, the gallery began to cheer, urging them on. Mickey reached out and rubbed Little Squire's neck. The tiny ears pricked toward the cheering crowd, flicked backward to catch Mickey's soft words of encouragement, and then pinned for a moment, as he gave a small buck and broke into a canter.

Mickey brought him around, and they picked up speed as they approached the mighty obstacle. Gathering everything he had, Little Squire sailed into the air and over the fence with room to spare. The crowd was on its feet, screaming, as Mickey and Little Squire trotted out of the arena, and My Play Boy entered. My Play Boy could not pull it off, and once again, the diminutive power-pony had made believers out of doubters. And he had given the crowd the thrill they'd been hoping for.

At the close of the show, the championship ribbon went to My Play Boy for overall points earned, but the next day, newspaper articles told only about the High Jump and the sensational Little Squire.

His reign of supremacy continued throughout that second summer with the Kennedys. In late August, at the Cohasset Show, he won first place in the Knockdown and Out, even after the jumps had been raised from three-foot-six to four-foot-nine. He won the Open Jumper sweepstakes, the only entrant to jump a clear round in that event. Eleven other full-sized horses could not manage the challenging course. Then, Little Squire thrilled the crowd in the Handy Horse Lunge Line competition.

The Lunge Line class, a riderless event in which the horse is judged on willingness, form, and jumping ability, was an easy event for Little Squire. The jump was challenging, a pole fence more than six feet high, but Little Squire made it look like a walk in the park. He not only won the class, but entertained the crowd with his usual flare and sense of fun.

Instead of keeping him on the lunge line (a long lead normally used for training horses), Mickey turned Little Squire loose in the ring. The spectators were perplexed. What was Mickey doing? Little Squire knew. He cantered around the arena, unguided, approached the fence with impeccable form, and then cleared the enormous jump with grace and ease. The applause was deafening. A photograph in the local paper captured the relaxed and winning jump – Little Squire with ears pricked forward, legs tucked in perfect form, looking every bit the champion that he was by the end of the show.

7

Retirement and Onward Glory

Little Squire's fans were now speculating about what would happen in the upcoming Nationals. Would he steal the November honors again? The great event was only two months away, and Little Squire seemed better than ever. Unknown to the public, though, changes were taking place at Audwill Stables.

The Kennedys, under Mickey's guidance, had become involved in steeplechasing. Over the past years, as they had in the jumping arena, they had established themselves as successful in the sport. They had reached a point where they had to choose which sport to put their efforts into. Steeplechasing won out, being far more lucrative and manageable.

Mickey had always loved the sport of steeplechasing and had an interest in a few horses of his own at the time. He agreed to stay on as the Kennedys' manager and trainer. It was decided that the show horses would be put up for sale, except for Audrey's favorite, Erin's Son. Mickey hated the thought of saying good-bye to Little Squire, but there was nothing to be done. The change was being made, and their time together would soon end.

Little Squire performed before a crowd of over four thousand spectators at his last major event, the Boston Horse Show, in early October of 1940. The crowd filled the Commonwealth Armory seats to capacity and crowded the standing space. There would be no faltering this year. Little Squire's performances over the three-day event were faultless and spectacular, and when he was led into the ring to receive the Open Jumper Championship, the spectators rose to their feet for a standing ovation.

The little white pony, son of a pretty little Connemara mare and great, gray thoroughbred stallion, stood statue still, only his ears moving as they flicked toward one side of the arena and then the other. His dark, bright eyes were shining. Mickey smiled and spoke quietly to him as the crowd cheered on.

Before presenting the championship award, the judge announced that this had been Little Squire's final event and that he would be going into retirement. The enormous crowd fell silent as the words were spoken, and then a low murmur swept the arena, a whisper of disbelief. The applause was half-hearted as the Championship ribbon was attached to Little Squire's bridle. But then, the unexpected got them back on their feet.

Mickey reached over and hugged Little Squire, then quickly detached the reins from his bridle and whispered, "Go out with a bang, Squire. Don't let 'em forget you." Mickey left the arena and closed the gate behind him.

As he had done the year before at the Nationals, Little Squire hesitated a moment, surveying the hushed crowd. This time, though, instead of galloping straight for the gate, Little Squire cantered around the arena, jumped several of the jumps, riderless and effortlessly, and then with a squeal, he galloped to the closed gate. As he soared over it, the crowd erupted and, for the last time, the sound of cheers and wild applause followed Little Squire and Mickey to the quiet of the stable.

*　　*　　*

Two weeks later, a man named Mr. William Gibbs approached the Kennedys and made an offer to buy Little Squire. The Kennedys had had several offers in the past weeks, some of them for substantial amounts of money, but all had been refused. Everyone who had approached them had wanted to compete with the pony, arguing that he was obviously still in top form and not ready to end his career. Everyone wanted a little piece of the glory that was Little Squire.

But Mickey insisted on a full retirement from the show scene. "Let him be remembered as the best there ever was," he said. The Kennedys agreed, and refused to sell Little Squire for show purposes.

Mr. Gibbs had a young son who was completely infatuated with Little Squire and had been following his career loyally. He was not interested in showing the pony, but hoped to have him as his own saddle horse to use on the family's estate on Long Island. He promised to give him the best of care for the rest of his days.

Mr. Gibbs and his son were sent to speak to Mickey. Although the pony was officially theirs, Audrey and William knew Little Squire truly belonged to Mickey. No sale would take place without his approval.

Mickey was friendly, but somewhat solemn during the meeting. His characteristic grin never broke the surface, and he kept a protective hand on Little Squire the whole time. They talked and visited for over an hour before Mickey offered the boy a chance to ride Little Squire. It was a good sign. Mickey was pleased by the boy's lightness of hand and solid seat. He didn't miss it when the boy made subtle adjustments to ensure Little Squire's comfort. He made his final decision when the boy hugged Little Squire at the end of the ride. The pony nickered softly to him and nudged him in the chest with his head – a gesture he normally reserved exclusively for young Kathleen. Mickey knew then, that this was a good fit.

Mickey, himself, delivered the pony to the Long Island estate, and he stayed for the afternoon to speak further to the boy about Little Squire's care. He wanted to be absolutely sure that Little Squire would live out his days in comfort and good health. When the time came to finally part, Mickey stroked Little Squire's neck and stood quietly, resting his forehead against the pony's.

"You're a hellava leaper, old man. God bless." And without looking back, he left.

It is believed that Little Squire spent the rest of his life on the estate, occasionally appearing at minor shows, but mainly returning to the more leisurely life that he had known as a colt. He was loved and well cared for until the end of his days by the boy who truly admired his greatness, as had so many thousands of others.

Mickey Walsh went on to be one the most respected and influential horsemen of his time. After moving with the Kennedys to Southern Pines, North Carolina, he gradually established his own stable – Stoneybrook. Stoneybrook became a major steeplechasing institution, and Mickey was held in greater esteem than ever before. He held the nation's leading steeplechase trainer award for five years straight (1950–1955), and became the third steeplechase trainer to win over a million dollars. He won the F. Ambrose Clark award in 1975, the sport's highest honor, given to a person who makes a significant contribution to steeplechasing. He was inducted into five halls of fame and continued to excel until his death, at the age of eighty-six. With him, through it all, were his wife, Kitty, his seven children, and the memory of his lost son, Thomas.

Mickey Walsh accomplished many wonderful things, but his time with Little Squire will always shine in a special light. Two talented Irish immigrants took New York by storm in a way no other pair could ever have done. They will never be forgotten.

About the Author

Judy Andrekson grew up in Nova Scotia with a pen in one hand and a lead rope in the other. At the age of twenty, she moved to Alberta, where she could pursue her great love of horses, and there she worked for six years, managing a thoroughbred racehorse farm. By her thirties, Judy had also begun to write seriously. Now she combines both of her passions in her new series for young readers, True Horse Stories. Judy also works as an educational assistant. She, her husband, and their daughter live in Sherwood Park, Alberta with a constantly changing assortment of animals.

True HORSE Stories by Judy Andrekson: